WRITING DIALOGUE

WRITING LESSONS FROM THE FRONT, BOOK 13

ANGELA E. HUNT

Other Lessons in the **Writing Lessons from the Front**
1. *The Plot Skeleton*
2. *Creating Extraordinary Characters*
3. *Point of View*
4. *Track Down the Weasel Words*
5. *Evoking Emotion*
6. *Plans and Processes to Get Your Book Written*
7. *Tension on the Line*
8. *Writing Historical Fiction*
9. *The Fiction Writer's Book of Checklists*
10. *Writing the Picture Book*
11. *The First Fifty Pages of your Novel*
12. *The Art of Revision*
13. *Writing Dialogue*

A Christian Writer's Possibly Useful Ruminations on a Life in Pages,
supplemental volume

Visit Angela Hunt's website at www.angelahuntbooks.com.
Dialogue, Copyright 2024, Angela Hunt.
Published by Hunt Haven Press. All rights reserved. Do not reproduce or share these pages without permission from the publisher.

ISBN: 978-1961394-810

CHAPTER ONE

Dialogue is like jazz. Dialogue is creative. —*Sam Shepherd*

Dialogue is the element that can make your novel sizzle. That can make your reader laugh. And can keep people from skimming page after page.

Why do people slow down to read dialogue? Because we humans are inherently nosy, and we want to know what other people are saying. Even if they're fictional characters.

What follows are some tips, guidelines, and caveats about writing dialogue. I tried to order them in a logical manner, but good dialogue isn't always logical or ordered.

So here they are, a few dialogue guidelines, stripped down to the important principles.

Enjoy the reading . . . then go have a conversation with your characters.

In real life, people fumble their words. They repeat themselves and stare blankly off into space and don't listen properly to what other people are saying. I find that kind of speech fascinating but screenwriters never write dialogue like that because it doesn't look good on the page. —Christopher Guest

What is good dialogue?

Writing dialogue should be easy, right? All you have to do is type what your characters say as they perform on the stage in your mind. Doesn't that create realistic dialogue?

In a word, no. Real people hem and haw, they say all sorts of things that have nothing to do with their conversational intent, and they ramble. But you don't want all that hemming and hawing on your pages.

Good dialogue is *approximate* speech. It creates *as much force as possible with as few words as possible.*

In this writing lesson, we're going to look at dialogue—what it can do and what it should do. We'll note some common but ineffective uses of dialogue and point out better ways to make dialogue work for your story.

Ready? Open your work-in-progress and find a passage of dialogue. Now listen to it.

Listen to Your Dialogue

I am going to assume that you've already worked on a rough draft of your novel, short story, or screenplay. Now that you're ready to edit and evaluate, don't read your dialogue aloud, let the computer read it to *you*. By listening, you will notice things you might have missed as you read your dialogue on the page.

If you work on a Mac computer, speech capability is

built in. If you work with Windows, use the Narrator to read your text aloud.

Does your dialogue sound like natural speech? Do your characters use contractions, occasional run-on sentences, and do they sometimes contradict each other? Real people do. And while it's true that dialogue is an *approximation* and not real speech, a lot of beginners' dialogue is neither.

Consider this:

"Hi, Bob. How are you?"

"Just fine, thanks. And you? How're the wife and kids?"

"Well, Marge had the flu, as you probably know, and Billy needs braces. Plus we just found out the roof leaks, so we'll be needin' to raid the savings account again, and that's a bummer but life's tough all over, right? Seems like we just can't get ahead."

"Well, it's nothing to be ashamed of. Everyone goes through tight spots—like last year when our septic tank got clogged. Talk about a mess! Wait—let me check my phone, I've got a message . . . Oops, I've gotta run. See you later."

"Nice seeing you."

"Yeah, you too."

Snooze-a-rama! Heaven help us if all books were written like that.

First, see those routine greetings? The "how are you"s and "See you laters?" Get rid of them; they're accomplishing nothing. You could just as easily write:

Bob and Tom met at the corner. After greeting Tom, Bob looked his friend in the eye and asked if he was having financial difficulties.

"Why would you ask that?"

Bob shrugged. "It's nothing to be ashamed of. Everyone goes through tight spots."

See what I mean? Cut to the chase almost every time. Those little pleasantries mean nothing—unless they're highly unusual and you want the reader to notice how unskilled a character is with typical pleasantries.

When you listen to your dialogue, see how long it takes your characters to get to the point. You may need to shorten that distance.

PUT the emotion in the writing, not in the speaker attributions

When you listen to dialogue, be grateful for the computer's slightly robotic voice. As you wrote your draft, you heard emotion in your characters' voices. The emotion will not be in the robotic computer voice, so you must put it in the words. If that emotion is only in your head, the reader is going to miss it.

If someone is angry, let him speak harsh words. If your character is happy, let his words—and his body language—reflect that emotional state. Make him smile, indicate that his voice has a pleasant lilt, let his eyes sparkle—just be sure you don't violate point of view. If Bob is the point of view character in that scene, he can't see his eyes sparkle, but he could feel as if he were about to burst with happiness.

RELAX the grammar rules in dialogue

When you're writing dialogue, you can ease up on the grammar rules and not worry so much about cutting weasel words. (If this means nothing to you, check out *Track Down the Weasel Words*, book four in the **Writing Lessons from the Front** series.) Clean up your narrative sections, but when your characters speak, let them talk like their natural selves. Sometimes they'll be so flustered they don't care about grammar. Sometimes their carefully-constructed facades will break down. Sometimes those hidden Southern accents will come out. Let your characters reveal themselves through their speech.

I know what a challenge it is to make your characters speak in different voices—most writers find that their characters talk like they do! (At least that's true for me.) If your characters are from the same social class, geographical area, and educational level, the challenge is even tougher.

As you write your characters' interior monologue and dialogue, remind yourself of each individual character's background, education, job, and life experience. Does he have an accent? Does she use words that carry over from her job? A person who has been to college is more apt to use multi-syllable words than someone who hasn't, and someone who uses a great deal of specialized terms in his job is likely to carry that vocabulary into his ordinary life.

So keep your character's ages, occupations, and education in mind when writing their dialogue. A seventy-year-old writer will know writing editorials for newspapers, but a twenty-something writer probably won't. An accountant will regularly use words like "accrue" and "fiduciary," but a gardener probably won't. A middle school kid will know all about the latest handheld video games, but his grandmother probably won't. A guy who graduated from Harvard may mention his alma mater several times a day in conversation, but someone who graduated from community college won't.

Some characters, like some people, have two or three

different ways of speaking. Barak Obama spoke in a very polished fashion when he addressed the nation or Congress, but he spoke in a more relaxed tone when he addressed black churches. Your character may speak one way at home with her family and use a more professional voice and tone when she's in a board meeting at her corporation.

If you can find the show, take a look at an old episode of *Gilligan's Island*. The setup: a handful of characters from wildly different social backgrounds were stranded on a desert island: the millionaire and his wife (who spoke "posh" English), a professor (who was always speaking in scientific terms), the skipper (who used a lot of nautical metaphors), the actress, the girl next door, and Gilligan. Each character had a particular way of speaking, dressing, and behaving. Can you make your characters as different as that crew?

It might help if you create a list of phrases or words your character uses habitually. Sprinkle those in and always make sure they are always applied to the same character.

I enjoy traveling to countries and towns where I set my books, and on my trips I always carry a little notebook. In it I jot any unusual (to me) word choices that I might be able to use in my novel. For instance, in the United States a sign on a stony hillside would say, "Watch for Falling Rocks." In Ireland, a similar sign said, "Mind Your Windscreen."

At Disney World, as you step off the monorail you hear, "Watch your step." In London, as you step out of the subway you hear, "Mind the gap."

In Ireland, I picked up little phrases like these:

- I tried to ring him
- He was a lovely man

- He was all of a dither
- He's a lovely little fella
- The cheek of him!
- He was obviously having me on

Having access to little conversation fillers like these can give your dialog loads of color.

One year three girlfriends and I spent a week in Ireland. For dinner one night, we slipped into a booth at an Irish pub and found ourselves sitting next to a booth occupied by a solitary man. He kept looking at us, so we politely said "Good evening," and one of my friends asked, "How are you?"

The man hung his head and said, "I'm pissed."

Trying to exhibit friendly concern, I said, "Why are you angry?"

He started to laugh. Then my friends laughed. And then I realized that the word I'd used didn't mean *angry* in Ireland, it meant *drunk*.

Ohhhhh . . . another phrase for my notebook.

Later, we told a cab driver about that little episode, and he said, "So he was chancin' his arm, eh?"

I'd never heard the phrase, but I got a sense of what he meant—risking a flirt—so that phrase went into the notebook, too. You can bet that both of those phrases and many others went into my Irish characters' conversations.

(By the way, I've since learned the origin of "chancin' his arm." Two ancient Irish families were feuding. After several skirmishes, one family locked themselves inside a church and were unwilling to come out lest they be slaughtered. So a man from the family *outside* the church had a hole cut in the church door and thrust his arm through it—knowing the other family could easily cut it off . The other family, recognizing his risk and his desire for peace, came out, thus ending the feud.)

Do some research into your characters' occupations—what are some words they would use in their daily work? How would those bleed into ordinary conversation? It's a great way to individualize your characters' speech.

I love a certain best-selling author, but one of his quirks drives me a little crazy. The writer has a brilliant vocabulary and so do his genius characters. Trouble is, his uneducated characters do as well, and their speech often strains my credibility.

Do your best to make sure your character dialogue matches your characters' educational level. Teenagers should talk like teenagers; professors like professors, children like children. If you plan on writing any children in the future, do yourself a huge favor and spend some time with kids. They don't talk like little adults, but neither do they speak entirely in one-syllable words.

Be careful with slang. Slang tends to come and go, so today's words may be dated tomorrow.

Also be careful with cultural references. I was baking with some twenty-somethings a few years ago, and I mentioned Barney Fife. I was met with blank faces. I didn't expect them to have watched the *Andy Griffith* show, but I thought surely they would have heard about Barney—he's a cultural icon! I was wrong.

The best dialogue springs from *character*. Our conversations reveal so much about us—our personality, our mindset, our educational level, our occupations, our attitudes . . . so use dialogue as a tool to further your character development. Make sure every word that spills from your characters' mouths is something 1) they would actually say and 2) something that defines their character.

. . .

As You Know, Bob

I remember watching one of the Muppet movies—I forget which one—and Kermit the Frog was talking to actress Diana Rigg. She was relating the long and convoluted history of several other characters when Kermit interrupted: "Excuse me—why are you telling me all this?"

She lifted one shoulder in an elegant shrug. "It's exposition. It has to go somewhere."

And away they went.

Don't be so obvious when you're delivering exposition. Do your best to find a creative way to impart information your reader needs to know.

But when you're writing, especially in the beginning when you are revealing your story world, watch out for the dreaded "As You Know, Bob." What's that?

Once I read a thriller about some people on a small island. One of the workmen told another, "Yes, Jim, I know we're stuck on this island with a ferry that only comes in the morning and in late afternoon . . ."

Whoa! Doesn't Jim know he's on an island? Doesn't he know when the ferry comes?

An "As You Know, Bob" is one character imparting information the other character would already know. I see this a lot on TV—one character will explain something (for the viewer, not for the other character's sake), and then the other character will say, "I know that."

What else could they say? But the viewer *also* knows the other character should know that, which makes for awkward dialogue.

If you absolutely *must* get some exposition across for your reader's sake, one of the most common methods is to have a newcomer show up—a new employee at the office. A new foster child in the family. An outsider with a mysterious past. None of these newcomers would know the town history, why Sally is an old grump, or the proper way to prepare for an autopsy, so one of the main characters can credibly fill them in, enlightening the reader/viewer as well. This effective tactic is frequently employed in books and films.

But keep one principle in mind: revealing too much information up front can kill the suspense of your story. The trick is to find the balance. Give enough information to keep the reader from becoming confused, but dole out other information only as needed.

Sometimes writing is like fishing—we toss out little hooks, or facts, to raise a question in the reader's mind and keeps them reading for the answer.

For instance, suppose Joe is walking newcomer Elijah through the town. They come upon Alice, who is sitting on the front porch of the general store . . . in chains.

> "That's ol' Alice," Joe said, flicking a thumb at the silent woman. "She's been chained up for years." He flashed a grin. "Did I tell you about the trout in our lake? Got some forty-pounders, I swear."

You don't have to explain *why* Alice is in chains, but Elijah—and your reader—is going to wonder. Let them wait for the explanation.

If you're writing a historical novel, you could provide background information by having a troubadour or mysterious stranger approach the campfire and tell a story in poetry or song. That's also dialogue, and it can be an effective way of telling the reader what you need him to know.

But whatever you do, don't have one character deliver an "As You Know, Bob" to another character. With just a little effort you can do so much better.

. . .

HISTORICAL DIALOGUE

We might as well admit it—the people of yesteryear spoke differently than we do today. Not only were their accents unlike ours, but their language was more formal—or less formal, depending upon whether you're writing about the founding fathers or cavemen.

If you insist on writing dialogue that sounds *exactly* like your characters would speak it, you may lose readers because few people have the patience to sift through dense, unfamiliar language. Never forget that we are a video generation. We have grown up with television and movies; we are accustomed to stories that flow on a screen in our imaginations. Consequentially, we tend to lack the patience of previous generations.

You can help your historical novel sound authentic by *sprinkling* the dialogue with common phrases from that time period. How to find them? Read documents written in your chosen era (Look for translations, if necessary). The more recent your chosen time period, the more documents you'll find available. For instance, when I wrote about the early American colonies I found several documents written by John White and his contemporaries. I gleaned these phrases from his letters and reports:

- I do beg and pray you
- Mind your manners, varlet
- Hold, sirrah
- Mark me
- Is aught amiss?
- I trow you could
- Pray do not tell
- Nothing of import
- Beshrew this
- A pox on him!

When I wrote about the ancient Egyptians, I found books of translated Egyptian poetry, and quoted some of the phrases in my novel. Reading works from your historical period will help you begin to think like your characters and become acquainted with some of their phrasing.

The historical novelist has to achieve a balance—you need to use enough historic dialogue to give a historic feel to your characters' voices, but you cannot be so authentic that you lose your modern reader.

I am currently writing a book set in first century Rome. I cannot write the book in Latin, of course, but I do try to sprinkle a few Latin terms throughout the story while making sure that their meaning is clear from context. The Romans' manner of speech was more formal than ours, so I use a little trick I've learned: I eliminate nearly all contractions from my characters' speech. Writing dialogue without contractions makes characters sound stilted and awkward, which sounds more like the formal dialogue of ancient people. While most of the words I use had not been invented in the first century, I try to avoid any words or terms that are clearly modern. I don't want to break the "fictive dream" and jerk my reader out of the story world by using a word that is clearly out of place . . . or time.

I have my ancient pagan characters swear by their gods (which they would have done), but I do not have them swear by the God of my readers (which would be offensive).

Anything that offends a reader's sensibility or breaks the fictive spell should be avoided. Historical novelist Stephanie Grace Whitson says, "I do not have my white people calling my black people what white people called black people back then. I do not have my white people thinking about my Lakota people what white people thought about Lakota people back then. And I certainly do not have my people (except the bad ones) *smell* like they smelled back then."

Novels are never completely realistic, and neither are films and TV. And no matter how much research we do, we who have been molded by twenty-first century events and culture may never fully understand the mindsets of previous generations.

I don't think a novelist can ever write a historical novel that is completely true to the period. We aim for verisimilitude and we strive to avoid contradicting historical fact, but we are keenly aware that we write for modern readers.

If you want your novel to reach the emotional core of your reader, keep her perceptions and attitudes in mind so she won't be ripped out of the story you're trying to tell. Write your characters' dialogue carefully, using historical terms, modern emotions, and find the balance between the past and present.

Don't write dialogue phonetically.

Years ago writers would approximate the sound of spoken speech by writing dialogue the way it sounded. Who can forget Mammy's speech in Margaret Mitchell's *Gone With the Wind?*

> "Ef you doan care 'bout how folks talks 'bout dis fambly, Ah does," she rumbled. "Ah ain' gwine stand by an' have eve'body at de pahty sayin' how you ain' fotched up right. Ah has tole you an' tole you dat you kin allus tell a lady by dat she eat lak a bird. An' Ah ain' aimin' ter have you go ter Mist' Wilkes' an' eat lak a fe'el han' an' gobble lak a hawg."

We don't write dialogue phonetically for several

reasons: it's hard to read, it breaks the fictive dream, and it's not politically correct. It's fine to drop a 'g' occasionally, or change *got to* to *gotta*, especially if it results in a more natural speech for your character, but please resist the urge to spell things the way they sound.

Instead of foisting strange spellings on your reader, indicate a dialect by word choice. For instance, an Irish woman might say, "Sure, and don't I know you're goin' with me?"

In her novel *The Help*, Kathryn Stockett did an amazing job of creating the sound and rhythm of southern black speech with word choice. Here's a paragraph from the first chapter:

> By the time she a year old, Mae Mobley following me around everywhere I go. Five o'clock would come round and she'd be hanging on my Dr. Scholl shoe, dragging over the floor, crying like I weren't never coming back. Miss Leefolt, she'd narrow up her eyes at me like I done something wrong, unhitch that crying baby off my foot. I reckon that's the risk you run, letting somebody else raise you chilluns.

By sprinkling a particular character's conversation with unique phrases—whether picked up in another country, another profession, or another social group—you will singularize that character. Soon your readers will know which character is speaking by the words he uses . . . or so we hope. Creating particular and unique characters is one of our goals as writers.

One way to show that a contemporary character's native language is *not* English is to eliminate all the contractions from his dialogue. The dialogue then becomes stiff, just as it would if the character was not skilled with English. But don't remove contractions from the dialogue of *all* your characters or they'll all sound stiff!

DIALOGUE IS *the most fun to write. It's kind of like a tennis match.* —Sally Rooney

No Ping Pong **Allowed**

If you look carefully at your dialogue, you may find that you are writing "on the nose"—with no subtlety or subtext. For every conversational "ping," the other character answers with an appropriate "pong."

Real conversation isn't like that . . . unless it's deadly boring.

Consider this:

> Tom carried the bag of groceries into the kitchen where Brenda waited.
>
> "Did you get the catsup?" she asked without looking up.
>
> "Yes, I did. Heinz. Because I know you like it."
>
> "I like any kind. As long as it's on sale."
>
> "Well, this one wasn't."
>
> "On sale?"
>
> "Right. But the mustard was twenty cents off. And by the way, I saw Melissa standing over in produce."
>
> "Melissa?" Brenda finally lifted her gaze. "Did she speak?"
>
> "Sure she did. She said hi and I said hi and then she asked if I'd seen Toby."
>
> "Well?"
>
> "I hadn't seen Toby."

"Did you tell her that?"

"Well, she asked, didn't she?"

That exchange has only one unexpected line (about Melissa). Let's try again.

> Tom carried the groceries into the kitchen where Brenda waited.
>
> "Catsup?" she asked without looking up.
>
> "Heinz. Because you won't eat anything else."
>
> "I like any kind, as long as it's on sale."
>
> "I saw Melissa standing over in produce."
>
> "Was it?" She turned, finally. "Was the catsup on sale?"
>
> "Did you hear me? I saw Melissa." He bent closer to look into her eyes. "She asked if I'd seen Toby."
>
> Brenda blinked. "You must think I'm some kind of tightwad."
>
> Tom slammed his fist onto the counter. "Good grief, Brenda, how long are you going to ignore that missing kid?"

Ah . . . much better. The first passage is an exercise in predictability; the second simmers with suspense. There are undercurrents and questions are flying through the reader's mind. Why is Brenda so concerned about the cost of catsup? Who's Melissa, and why doesn't Brenda want to hear about her? Why is Tom so upset? And who in the heck is Toby?

(I don't know the answers to any of those questions. If you do, feel free to finish the story.)

So don't let your dialogue click back and forth like a metronome. Like a professional tennis match, let the players return the ball for a while, then miss a shot.

Keep the dialogue off-balance, and you'll keep your

characters off-balance. Keep your characters off-balance and you'll keep your readers off-balance. And that's a good thing because it add tension to any novel.

There's yet another aspect to "on the nose" writing—which we are supposed to avoid. Not only should we not ping pong, we should avoid saying exactly what our characters are thinking. Sometimes the *words left unsaid* are the most powerful.

Sometimes NO dialogue is the best dialogue

I used to be obsessed with the TV show *Alias*, about CIA operatives. Never watched it on TV, but I rented the DVDs and became enthralled by the writing. There was never a dull moment, never a plot thread wrapped up without another one being strung out.

Anyway, in season one (I think) Vaughn and Sydney are being attracted to each other. We know Vaughn wants to declare his feelings, but is he going to greet Sydney with a fervent "I think I love you?" Of course not. That would be *on the nose writing*. Too easy and too obvious.

So there's a scene where they're together and Vaughn shows Sydney a watch--the watch his much-admired-and-killed-in-the-line-of-duty-father gave to him. "You see this watch?" he says. "My dad gave it to me. He said you could set your heart by this watch.'

Sydney looks at him, waiting.

Vaughn continues: "The thing is, this watch stopped on October first. That's the day we met."

And Sydney looks at him and smiles and says,"Me, too."

And we get it. He's really saying, "My heart stopped on the day we met," and she replies, "Me, too." She's not talking about the watch. She's talking about her heart.

Why is this great dialogue? Because it's unexpected and

it's not on the nose. It's not tit for tat. Sydney responds to what he's thinking, (*I think I love you*), not what he's saying.

I saw another great exchange not long after the scene above. Sydney and Vaughn were together, and Syd confessed that she lied to Vaughn about a co-worker. She says she pretty much grew up alone, so she's not used to being accountable to someone, and she's sorry she lied to him.

And Vaughn cocks a brow and you're not sure if he's going to be angry or forgiving or hurt or irritated . . . but he offers her a bite of his ice cream, then he stands and offers her his hand. Invisible dialogue, pure sentiment, not cliche sentimentality. He's saying, "I forgive you. I still want to share my life with you." And he did it all without saying a word.

Most of us have a little writer in us that is constantly predicting what a character will say--and in a lot of movies and TV shows, I find myself parroting dialogue right along with the characters because the setup and following lines are so predictable. I've never been able to do that with *Alias*. And that's a delight.

CHAPTER TWO

AS FOR DIALOGUE, I THINK IT KEEPS THINGS MOVING TO CUT to the chase. —Jerry B. Jenkins

SPEAKING OF SUSPENSE...

A lot of beginning writers think adding suspense means plotting a murder and throwing in a lot of exclamation points. But unless a character's house is on fire or he's running for his life, you'll want to lose that excessive punctuation. Too many exclamation points come across as amateurish—as though you're working too hard to convey a sense of urgency. So reserve them for truly dire circumstances, if you use them at all.

Find more elegant ways to convey emotion or urgency through dialogue, interior monologue, or action. And remember—sometimes an emotion is stronger if it's understated. Quiet can be intense.

Scene: Sherry's six-year-old daughter is missing when Sherry tries to pick her up from school.

Somehow Sherry found herself in the school office, where what seemed like dozens of people offered her a seat and a glass of water. Why wouldn't they offer something useful?!

The principal, Mrs. Jones, hurried into the room, breathing hard. "I've just spoken to your daughter's teacher," she said, planting her arm on the tall counter. "And she says a man picked your daughter up ten minutes ago. She assumed he was your husband."

"My husband is dead!" Sherry heard the words rip from her own throat. "And Lily wouldn't go with anyone else because I've taught her about stranger danger. Someone has taken her! She's been kidnapped!"

"Mrs. Smith, I'm sure there's a logical explanation—"

"You don't know what you're talking about!" In blind panic, Sherry turned and ran from the office.

That's certainly one approach—and one where exclamation points could be justified. But take a moment to consider the opposite approach:

Somehow Sherry found herself in the school office, where what seemed like dozens of people offered her a seat and a glass of water. Why wouldn't they offer something useful? Why wouldn't one of them calmly step forward and explain where Lily was, and how there'd been a simple misunderstanding—

The principal, Mrs. Jones, hurried into the room, breathing hard. "I've just spoken to your daughter's teacher."

"Lily," Sherry said, her voice muffled by the pounding of blood in her ears. "Her name is Lily."

"Of course." Mrs. Jones made an effort to smile. "The teacher says a man picked Lily up ten minutes ago. She assumed he was your husband."

Sherry stared as the room shifted. "My husband—" her voice faltered—"my husband died four years ago. In Afghanistan."

"I'm so sorry." The principal pressed her hand to her ample chest. "Let me find you a place to sit. I'm sure you want to make some calls to see if Lily could have gone home with one of her friends or—"

Sherry cut her off with an uplifted hand. "My daughter is missing, so I'm going to call the police." She stood, then clutched the counter as her knees buckled. "I'm fine," she whispered. "Or I will be when I find Lily."

You may disagree, but I find the second scene more powerful—and it doesn't have a single exclamation point.

How do you create tension through dialogue? Have your characters express their fear and uncertainty. Let us see their vulnerability. And keep the reader wondering if everything is, in fact, going to be fine.

THERE IS a tendency to underestimate the power of what we can do without words. Sometimes you can make a scene even more powerful and precise without dialogue. —Mads Mikkelsen

SUBTEXT

The other night I was watching a British TV show. The episode opened with a man and his wife in their kitchen, and from their facial expressions I knew the situation was tense. She said something like "This is my first day at work—and you choose this time to tell me?"

He said, "We'll talk about it later."

"I want to know *who*," she said. "And I want to know *why*."

"We'll talk later." He moved toward the door.

She caught his arm. "We need to talk now."

He shook himself free. "*I have to go.*"

And in that moment, I knew he was saying two things: not only did he have to leave for work, he also had to leave the marriage.

The screenwriters didn't have to spell anything out. From the actors' expressions and the brief snippets of dialogue we viewers understood that he had just told his wife he was leaving her because he had fallen in love with someone else.

No wordy explanations at all. But loads of tension, and in the husband's last line, loads of subtext.

Subtext in dialogue is a wonderful way to raise tension. As I've already mentioned, many beginning writers create "on the nose" dialogue in which each character answers the other precisely as expected. Strong dialogue has unexpected beats and responses. Subtext in dialogue—in which the characters speak more loudly through their actions and attitudes than through their words—is a wonderful source of tension.

Do an Internet search for "Hills Like White Elephants" by Ernest Hemingway—you're certain to find it online. This is a simple short story, ostensibly about a man and a woman drinking beer at an outdoor café in Spain.

They chat about the hills, about the beer, and then the conversation takes a turn:

> 'It's really an awfully simple operation, Jig,' the man said.
> 'It's not really an operation at all.'
>   The girl looked at the ground.

'I know you wouldn't mind it, Jig. It's really not anything. It's just to let the air in.'

The girl did not say anything.

'I'll go with you and I'll stay with you all the time. They just let the air in and then it's all perfectly natural.'

'Then what will we do afterwards?'

'We'll be fine afterwards. Just like we were before.'[1]

Reading between the lines, a savvy reader understands that the woman is pregnant and the man is talking about an abortion. The word *abortion* is never used, neither are the words *baby* or *fetus*. But at this point the tension begins to rise, because the reader wonders why the man wants her to have an abortion and what decision the woman will make. Another question rises further down the page—what did the woman ever see in this man?

The conversation continues, and we realize the man is completely selfish, not wanting to have to share the woman with anyone else, not even a child. She finally begs him to stop talking.

At the story's end, after the man has taken their bags to the train and spent a little time drinking at the bar, he returns to the woman.

'Do you feel better?' he asked.

'I feel fine,' she said. 'There's nothing wrong with me. I feel fine.'

In an ever-so-subtle line, Hemingway lets us know the woman will keep the baby. She doesn't need an operation, and she won't have one. The reader's questions are finally answered.

After you've completed a first draft of your manuscript, print it out, stack the pages neatly, and then pull a page at random from the pile. Read what you've written with pen in hand, and highlight any line or passage that raises a question in the reader's mind. If you've written a page of pleasant description or genial conversation and you find nothing to highlight, it's time to rewrite.

Tension doesn't require bombs and bullets, arguments or spooky encounters. It requires questions without immediate answers.

"But I'm writing narrative," you may be thinking. "I'm writing a simple scene to move my character from one place to another. There's no confrontation, no real drama. Do I really need tension on this page?"

You do . . . unless you want your reader to skip those pages or put your book down.

To create tension in dialogue, make sure tension exists between the conversing people and is not necessarily part of their topic. Two people may converse about a political opinion they share, but if they don't like each other, sparks can fly.

Example: Tom, Larry's friend and boss, has ordered Larry to ask all the guys at the warehouse to contribute to the Fund for Orphans, a group they both support. Larry carries the donations to Tom's office and drops the container on his boss's desk.

> Tom looked up, a spark of irritation in his eye. "What's this?"
>
> Larry pressed his lips together. "You know. You asked me to badger the guys for money; here it is. All sixty-seven dollars and twenty-three cents."
>
> "That's all?"
>
> "Money's tight now, at least for us working stiffs. The guys on the floor don't earn anywhere close to what you administrative fat cats get."

Tom sniffed, then lifted the rusty coffee can and set it on his open palm, as if weighing it. "For the record, I didn't ask you to badger anybody. And you should remember who you're calling a fat cat."

Larry exhaled. "Can I go?"

"You got some place to be?"

Larry wanted to answer that he'd rather be alone on the dark side of the moon with a severe rash than in this room, but that response would get him a scowl and a fifteen-minute lecture.

"Yeah," he finally said, sliding his hands into his pockets. "I got some place to be."

Tom lifted a brow as a wicked gleam entered his eye. "You dog," he drawled, a lascivious smile crawling across his face. "Get out of here, then. Go get 'er, whoever she is."

"I'm going home . . . to my wife."

Larry left the office, reflexively wiping his hands on his jeans. Lately every time he left Tom's office, he felt like he needed a shower.

But he wouldn't have to suffer Tom much longer.

What questions did that scene raise in your mind? Do you want to know what happened between these two? What event or circumstance accounts for the barely-tempered hostility between them?

And what's going to happen to Tom? Has Larry arranged a hit or something?

I'd read more to find out.

―――

Profanity

Before we discuss the effectiveness of profanity in

dialogue (or narrative, for that matter), let's define it. The dictionary definition is "blasphemous or obscene language." In other words, profanity is language that sullies something religious (from Latin roots meaning "outside the temple"). In common use, *profanity* includes any word that offends, including words that are profane, sexual, or scatalogical.

I don't use profanity in my writing. My villains occasionally curse, but I'm more likely to write, "He cursed" or "He turned the air blue" than to quote the actual words. I don't have to be specific to get my point across.

I know some writers enjoy flinging profanity around in an attempt to be realistic, but certain words are so overused that they no longer shock . . . though they can still offend.

Words that were powerful oaths in Shakespeare's day (Zounds!) don't offend most contemporary readers because we're unfamiliar with the word's meaning and connotation (Zounds: God's wounds, or swearing by Christ's wounds. Highly blasphemous). On the other hand, some words that offend today wouldn't have offended a previous generation because they wouldn't have understood the current meaning.

Here's the key: no matter what your personal conviction on profanity, you need to write *for your readers*.

Think about it—we don't use profanity when writing for children. Profanity in academic writing would be considered unprofessional. Ditto for profanity in legal briefs or public service announcements.

Not everyone reading this lesson will share my opinion, of course. But listen to Nathaniel Tower, another professional writer, one who *does* occasionally use profanity:

> Profanity also has virtually no place in academic or informative writing. No matter how many articles we read

about how people who use profanity might be smarter, no one ever sounds more intelligent when they say or write profane words. There has never been a time when an editor has asked me to add profanity, but there have been plenty of occasions where I've been asked to remove it.

Regardless of the type of writing you are doing, it's important to understand that using profanity won't instantly make your writing more appealing, and it definitely won't make you a better writer. Generally speaking, heavy use of profanity will always narrow the appeal of your writing. I've never heard anyone read a story and then say, "Wow, I really would have liked this book if it had more bad words." But I have seen plenty of situations where people complained about the amount of profanity in a book or movie (and not just from very conservative or "prudish" people)[2].

I know my readers—most of them are Christians and conservative. Even when I write suspense novels with *no* overt Christian content, I avoid profanity. You might be surprised to realize how many people appreciate a "clean" story.

My friend Athol Dickson, a fine novelist, has this to say about the subject of "realistic language:"

> Some people think "edgy" or "realistic" fiction means transcribing language exactly as it would be spoken in real life. They think this is necessary in order to show characters "as they really are." That is not good writing.
>
> After thinking about it further, I would now add the examples of dialect and accent. Of course we all know good writers don't transcribe speech exactly as a southerner or a Mainer or a recent immigrant might speak it. We pick a very few words and terms and use

them sparingly at opportune moments while translating all the others into standard English for the sake of readability.

Dialogue written as people truly speak it would require readers to rise out of the story to translate too many words. It would be unreadable. It is an unfair imposition on them. In a similar way, profanity drives the reader outside of the story *if* the reader is not accustomed to it, and *if* the reader believes such language is wrong, or offensive, or both.[3]

So consider carefully if profanity is worth the risk of offending readers or coming across as too lazy to think of another way to express a character's anger.

The FAS Rule

Believe it or not, there is a best way to order elements of feeling, action, and speech (dialogue).

Example: James is angry. He is going to say something and he is going to slam his hand on the desk. Which of these examples works best?

- "I hate her!" James slammed his hand on the desk as anger rose within him.
- James slammed his hand on the desk. "I hate her!" Anger rose within him.
- As anger rose within him, James slammed his hand on the desk. "I hate her!"

The emotion usually precedes the action and the dialogue, so order those elements with feeling first, action second, and speech last: FAS. And if you *really* want to write tight, since the anger is evident in the hand slamming, omit the first part of the sentence.

> James slammed his hand on the desk. "I hate her!"

In most situations, the FAS order works best.

Body Language

In communication, only 7 percent of understanding derives from what is actually spoken. Thirty-eight percent comes from tone of voice, and a whopping 55 percent comes from the silent speech signals otherwise known as body language.

You should get a book on basic body language and memorize a few poses. Most you will translate instinctively. For instance, someone who stands with their arms folded across their chest is literally erecting a wall between himself and the outside world. Arms folded plus fists clenched may signify anger behind the wall.

One arm folded and one arm hanging down is what I consider the typical "middle school" pose. The person wants to be relaxed and accepted, but the other arm is in a defensive position just in case. At a glance, this person looks awkward and unsure.

Men who stand with their feet apart and thumbs tucked into belt or waistband, fingers pointing toward the crotch —well, if you think about it, that posture is self-explanatory. It's what I think of as *cowboy cocky*.

A woman who plays with her hair in the presence of a man is literally preening—she's attracted to the man. If she sits on the sofa with a foot tucked beneath her, her bent knee will most likely be pointed toward a man who has piqued her interest. If she kicks off her shoe while in this pose, she's telegraphing her attraction to him.

A person who's insecure about a certain body part may touch it several times in the course of a conversation—a bald man may rub his head, for example. A liar may tug on his ear or rub his nose. He may avoid direct eye contact, but some liars can look anyone in the eye and utter the boldest fabrications imaginable.

A boss who comes out from behind his desk and sits on the edge to look down at his employee may be subtly pointing out that he is *over* the employee. That he's a "bigger" man. Or woman, as the case may be.

The man or woman who touches your arm while you're talking is asking to cut into the conversation. You may be talking too much.

What can you pick up from body language in this scene?

> Sylvia heard laughter from the next room. She had welcomed Charles and Melanie ten minutes before, and both said their respective spouses were on the way. "Harry always has to work late," Melanie had said, her lower lip protruding as she walked toward the living room, "but he'll make it."
>
> Sylvia put three glasses of iced tea on a tray, then paused beneath the plastered archway. Charles and Melanie were sitting on the sofa, but Melanie had turned toward Charles, one elbow on the back of the sofa as she played with strands of her long blonde hair.
>
> "Come on, Charlie," she purred. "Just give me your hand. I want to look at your lifeline."
>
> Sylvia snorted beneath her breath. If Charlie knew what was good for him, he'd move to the recliner.

Body language is not an exact science—a woman may have her arms folded because she's cold—but it's useful to writers because if you use it in your dialogue and scenes, the reader will subconsciously pick up on these cues. So don't add body language merely as beats to break up extended passages of dialogue; use them to help the reader see what's going on *beneath* the conversation.

Avoid Dinnertime Dialogue

I'm not saying you should never write a scene where people talk and eat at the same time. You can, but it can be tricky. I stumbled into writing a dinner table dialogue once, and I'll never do it again.

In my novel *The Canopy*, I wrote a scene where ten characters sat around a dinner table and discussed their upcoming expedition into the jungle. To make matters worse, the ten people were from different countries—a Russian, an Englishman, a couple of Americans, a Peruvian, a Frenchman, and others I've forgotten. Because it would have been beyond awful to end every bit of dialogue with "so-and-so said," I resorted to body language beats to make it clear who was speaking. So characters were casting looks, passing plantains, shrugging, dropping spoons, picking up spoons, waving forks, dropping napkins, retrieving napkins—well, you get the picture.

To make matters worse, my friend Bill Myers and I recorded the book for audio, using accents for each of the characters. Bill read all the male point of view scenes and dialogue, and I read all the female scenes and dialogue. But when we got to the dinner table scene, with all the characters talking at once, I think Bill was tempted to bash me over the head with the manuscript. Talk about a challenge!

So do yourself a favor—if at all possible, limit conversations in your book to two or three people at a time. You'll be glad you did. Besides, when you're at a banquet, who do you actually talk to? The people on either side of you, right? So it is natural to keep dialogue between *two or three people at a time*.

One day you'll thank me for that tip.

If I were to write that scene today, I'd mix dialogue with *described speech* and eliminate a lot of that body language. Something like this:

> Elliott passed Ginger the salt and pepper. "I'm eager to climb into the forest canopy tomorrow," he said. "Excited about the possibilities."
>
> Ginger said she'd been dreaming of the opportunity for months.
>
> "Years," Romonav said. "We have been waiting for years. The last time we discussed biophages—"
>
> "Plantains please," the guide said, looking bored.
>
> Elliot winked at Ginger and promised to race her to the top of the tree.

Much smoother and easier to read.

Speaker Attributions

In middle and high school, our English teachers rejoiced when we got jiggy with colorful speech attributions. We had characters chortling, laughing, chuffing, retorting, explaining, bellowing, and burping responses to one another. Our teachers smiled and called us creative.

If you try the same thing in professional writing, your work will be returned to you faster than a blink. When you write dialogue, whether in fiction or nonfiction, your best bet is to use the word *said* in speaker attributions. Better yet, don't use anything at all, but indicate who's speaking by occasional body movement.

Let's look at a sample that could be part of a nonfiction interview:

> I met up with the two cupcake bakers at their shop on East Avenue. Martha wore a blue apron, Bettye wore pink.
>
> "I always did like girly things," Bettye said, wiping the counter with practiced ease. "Martha's always liked blue."
>
> Martha swiped a stray hair out of her eyes. "I'm not a tomboy; don't you write that. I just like the sea, that's all. It seems cool, and it can get awful hot when you're standin' next to an oven."

In the first paragraph, I used the word *said* and it probably slid by without stirring even a ripple of recognition in your mind. *Said* is like the word *the*—it's almost invisible.

In the third paragraph, it's clear from the physical action (Martha swiping a hair out of her face) that this is going to be a Martha paragraph, so any dialogue that follows will come from her. No speaker attribution is needed.

When you're writing dialogue—whether it's in a polished professional article or in the funkiest fiction—try to avoid people growling, giggling, or gasping in their speaker attributions.

Dialogue Explanations

Another situation to avoid whenever possible is *dialogue that contains explanations*. Like this: "What's wrong?" she asked, confused.

The woman's confusion should be evident in her expression or in *what she said*, not in the writer's clumsy way of *telling* us she is confused. Remember the old adage *show, don't tell?* This may be brief telling, but it's still telling.

If you really want to add a bit more to emphasize her confusion, do it with description, not a speaker attribution.

> Her eyes clouded as she looked from Tom to Mary. "What's wrong? What aren't you telling me?"

Make sure the confusion is evident in the description and in the dialogue itself.

Dialogue Adverbs

The function of an adverb is to prop up a weak verb, so let's keep them out of speech attributions.

In an early draft of a novel, I once wrote:

> "No slave holder is ever going to sit at my table," Mrs. Haynes said emphatically.

Okay, all is forgivable in a first draft. Writing is revising; we know that. So we get rid of any adverb after *said*.

Said *emphatically*. Said *angrily*. Said *softly*. Said *impetuously*.

I could fill a page with said + adverbs, and they'd all be awful. Instead of *said softly,* write *whispered*. Said angrily? Yelled. (And a note of caution here—we don't want to go too overboard, lest we get into people screaming, roaring, screeching . . . you get the picture.)

As to my example, I ended up writing:

"No slave holder is ever going to sit at my table." Mrs. Haynes unfolded her napkin with an emphatic snap. "You can be assured of that."

Yes, it's more words, but I traded an adverb for a sensory detail—the snap of the napkin—and that's a trade well made.

I DO LOVE TO EAVESDROP. It's inspirational, not only for subject matter but for actual dialogue, the way people talk. —Lynda Barry

I WRITE FROM REAL LIFE. I am an unrepentant eavesdropper and a collector of stories. I record bits of overheard dialogue. —Chimamanda Ngozi Adichie

THE ART of Eavesdropping

So how do you discover bits of authentic dialogue for your fictional characters? One way is to develop the art of discreet eavesdropping. Go have a cup of coffee at a diner and read a book while you're sipping your java. Listen to the people in the booth behind you. Jot down things they say, paying particular attention to any unique words or phrases. You don't even have to look at the people (maybe it's best if you don't!), just listen to how they express themselves.

You can do this anywhere—while waiting in line, sitting in a doctor's office, or listening to phone-in callers on a radio station. Keep a notebook or recorder handy and keep notes of things you hear. If you can't carry a notebook, use the record feature on your phone to make a voice memo for later reference.

When I traveled in Ireland, I was quick to jot down any sayings or signs I could use to make my characters sound authentic. Do the same whenever you travel, no matter where you go. The language of Brooklyn is not the language of Atlanta or Savannah. You don't have to have your dialogue reflect every little nuance of a Brooklyn dialect (and remember, we shouldn't use a lot of funky spellings), but choose a few well-placed words to give a feeling of a real person from Brooklyn . . . or Savannah . . . or Little Havana in Miami.

Revealing **Character through Interior Monologue**

In James Collins's novel, *Beginner's Greek*, the protagonist studies a young woman who sits next to him on a plane:

> The young woman sat down. As well as he could, while pretending to idly look around the cabin, Peter studied her. She appeared to be about Peter's age, and she had long reddish blond hair that fell over her shoulders. She wore a thin, white cardigan and blue jeans. What Peter first noticed in her profile was the soft bow of her jaw and how the line turned back at her rounded chin. It reminded Peter of an ideal curve that might be displayed in an old painting manual. His eye traveled back along the jaw, returning to the girl's ear. It was a small ear, beige in color, that appeared almost edible, like a biscuit.

Nice description, isn't it? We get a fairly good picture of an attractive young woman, but in that paragraph we are getting a far better picture of Peter, the character who is thinking about the girl. (By the way, notice that there are no italics to indicate thought, nor are there any thought attributions like "he mused." Those are not needed when you're using point of view skillfully. Using third person, James Collins has taken us inside Peter's head, so we know we are reading Peter's thoughts. Using italics to indicate thought and switching to first person is an outmoded technique that's simply not necessary. Why switch POV and use an italic font when you can simply write what the character is thinking?)

From the paragraph above, we learn a great deal about Peter. What is his educational level? Clearly, he's been to college, probably an Ivy League school where he received a classical education. He is more likely to have studied Humanities than engineering. He knows about art. But most notably, he's attracted to this young woman . . . so attracted that he would like to nibble her ear lobe.

At another point, Peter visits an office and meets a secretary.

> Peter entered and the woman quickly rose to greet him. She was full-figured and in her fifties, with brassy red hair, black eyebrows, and one discolored front tooth. She made every utterance with great enthusiasm.

Notice that the author doesn't give us a string of details. We don't know what she's wearing, nor do we hear any of the exact words she says. Instead, the author chooses the details most likely to give us pertinent information. We read that the woman's red hair is "brassy," so we infer that it came from a home dye job. We read that she's "full-figured" instead of being "svelte," and she has black eyebrows—which do not match the red hair. But the most telling detail of all is the discolored front tooth. With that one element, the author—and Peter, as the point of view character—reveals that this woman most likely did not go to college and this is the best job she can get. She can't afford to get the tooth fixed, and she is not relaxed on the job, so she's making every utterance "with great enthusiasm."

I don't know about you, but I feel sorry for the woman. I'm also a little annoyed with Peter for pointing out her flaws.

Interior monologue—what a character thinks—is a sort of dialogue. Make sure it also reflects your character's vocabulary, personality, social standing, and occupation. The character's inner voice should remain consistent, unless he or she *intends* to mislead people with his or her spoken speech.

What comes easiest for me is dialogue. Sometimes when my characters are speaking to me, I have to slow them down so that I'm not simply taking dictation. —Richard Russo

Revealing **Character Through Dialogue**

The following is from the first scene of my novel, *The Offering*. I have omitted some of the narrative bits.

> Marilee and I were trying to decide whether we should braid her hair or wear it in pigtails when Gideon thrust his head into the room. Spotting me behind our daughter, he gave me a look of frustrated disbelief. "Don't you have an important appointment this morning?"
>
> Shock flew through me as I dropped the silky brown strands in my hands. Of course, this was Monday. At nine

I had a tremendously important interview with the Pinellas County school system. How could I have let time slip away from me on such an important day?

"Gideon!" I yelled toward the now-empty doorway. "Can you call Mama Isa and tell her I'll be late this morning?"

"Just get going," he yelled, exasperation in his voice. "Your coffee's in the kitchen."

I squeezed Marilee's shoulders. "I'm sorry, sweet girl, but this morning we have to go with something quick."

"Okay. Can I wear it like Princess Leia tomorrow?"

I frowned, trying to place the name. "How does Princess Leia wear her hair?"

"You know." Marilee held her hands out from her ears and spun her index fingers in circles. "She has honey buns on her ears."

I laughed, placing the image—the princess in *Star Wars*. "Sure, if you want to have honey buns over your ears, that's what we'll do."

I pulled the long hair from the top of her head into a ponytail, looped an elastic band over it, and tied a bow around the band. Then I kissed the top of her head and took a moment to breathe in the sweet scent of her strawberry shampoo. "Love you."

She grinned. "Love you, too."

Twenty minutes later I stood in my closet, wrapped in a towel and dripping on the carpet. What to wear? I had a nice blue skirt, but the waistband had lost its button and I had no idea where I'd put it. The black pantsuit looked expensive and professional, but sand caked my black sandals because I wore them to the beach last weekend.

"Baby girl?"

"In here."

The closet door opened and Gideon grinned at me, a

fragrant mug in his hand. "Are you ever going to learn how to manage your schedule?"

I grabbed the mug and gulped a mouthful of coffee. "Maybe I like living on the edge."

"And Mama says *I* have a dangerous job." He waggled his brows at the sight of my towel. "Pity you don't have any extra time this morning."

"And too bad you have to get Marilee to school. So off with you, soldier, so I can get my act together."

Chuckling, Gideon lifted his hands and stepped away from the closet. "Okay, I'm heading out. But you're picking up our little bug from school today, right?"

I dropped the blouse I'd been considering. "I'm *what*?"

"You have pickup duty because I'm leading a training exercise."

For an instant his face went sober and dark, reminding me of the reason he'd been so busy lately. The military had to be planning something, an operation Gideon couldn't explain to a civilian.

"Sure." My voice lowered. "I've got it covered."

He nodded, but a hint of uncertainty lingered in his eyes. "Mandy—"

"I've got it." I shooed him out the door. "Tell Marilee I'll see her later."

No bomb blasts in this opening, just a husband and wife trying to get themselves and their daughter out the door one morning. But what have you learned about Mandy from her dialogue?

What kind of mother is she? Does she have a sense of humor? What kind of wife is she? What kind of marriage do she and Gideon share? Do they share responsibilities equally? Is Mandy exceptionally well-organized or is she one of those people who is more relaxed about daily activities?

Dialogue, narrative, and interior monologue (thoughts) work together to reveal character by showing and not telling.

REVEALING Character through the Eyes of Others

Sometimes you can reveal a character by prodding another character to talk about him. You need to be careful, though, lest this technique become too obvious. You don't want his opinion to become an "As-you-know-Bob," as in this example:

> Leaning over the bench, Tom addressed Bob. "You seen Charlie today?"
>
> Bob nodded. "Saw him over at the clubhouse bar, as per usual."
>
> "I'm afraid Doug has it in for him." Tom drew a deep breath, then exhaled it through his teeth. "As you know, Charlie has a quick temper. Remember last fall when he decked that caddy? I was afraid Doug had hit his limit then, but this has to be the last straw. "
>
> Bob dipped his chin in a slow nod. "Doug's wife always did like them zinnias."
>
> "'Fraid so. And runnin' 'em over was the worst thing Charlie could have done."
>
> Bob picked up the glove that had fallen from the top of his bag. "Looks like our foursome is gonna become a threesome."

Having two characters tell each other things they already know is silly. But if you can get rid of the obvious statements, you can easily have Tom and Bob reveal Charlie's personality traits through dialogue. After removing that "as-you-know" phrase, the above paragraph would do a fine job of telling us that Charlie has a temper and probably a drinking problem, too. (Would you run over a woman's prize zinnias if you were *sober*?)

Prayers

I often get questions from writers about prayers—how do you format them? Are they dialogue? Should you even use them?

If your character prays—regularly or occasionally—of course you should use them. If they are spoken, they should naturally be placed inside quotation marks. "Lord, get me out of here" is a verbalized prayer, so write it as you'd write any line of dialogue.

Prayers that are internal thoughts could be italicized to set them off from the character's other thoughts, but try to keep them brief. Italics aren't easy to read, especially when used for an entire paragraph, so keep those silent prayers brief or break them up into snatches.

Like this:

> Terrified by the approaching shadow, she sought the words to the prayer her mother had always recited: *Our Father, who art in heaven, hallowed be thy name. Thy kingdom come, thy will be done, on earth as it is in heaven. Give us this day our daily bread and forgive us our trespasses, as we forgive those who trespass against us. And lead us not into temptation . . .*

Much easier (and more interesting) to read this way:

Terrified by the approaching shadow, she sought the words to the prayer her mother had always recited: *Our Father, who art in heaven . . .*

Footsteps echoed in the empty hallway.

Thy kingdom come, thy will be done—

The shadow hesitated, turned.

On earth as it is—dear God, please don't let this man kill me!

If our characters pray, God will often respond, sometimes with words. How do you write God's side of the dialogue?

If He has answered with spoken words, use quotes.

After pouring my heart out, I waited for a sign—a change in the wind, a burst of birdsong, something, an inexplicable scent—then I heard His answer:

"Go find your mother."

I glanced around, certain I'd see a man hiding in the bushes or some teen pranking me, but I was completely alone.

"Go find your mother."

The voice was patient, earnest, and calm. Just like that, I'd prayed and God answered.

Imagine.

If the words aren't spoken, you could always use italics or even boldface to emphasize the supernatural dimension of the conversation. But whatever you do, remember that italics and boldface are for *emphasis*, not entire conversations.

Punctuation in Dialogue

You may think I'm being picky when I bring up em dashes and ellipses, but if you want your manuscript to rise above the average submission in the slush pile, you should apply these punctuation marks properly.

First, know what they are. An *em dash* is a long hyphen: —. If you type two hyphens in most word processing programs, the auto correct will automatically insert an em dash (unless that feature has been turned off).

You use em dashes in a couple of ways. First, you can use an em dash to insert a parenthetical phrase.

Example: All manuscripts—including this one—need to be proofread.

Just be sure to use an em dash at the beginning and the end of the inserted phrase. Lots of writers make the mistake of using an em dash at the beginning and a comma where the second em dash should go.

Another use for an em dash, particularly in fiction, is to indicate when someone has been interrupted.

> "Let me tell you a story," Grandpa said, settling back in his chair. "It all began when your grandma went out to butcher a hog. She had no sooner—"
>
> "Come and eat," Grandma called from the kitchen. "Last one in has to hear the end of that silly story."

In nonfiction, an ellipsis (. . .) is used to indicate the omission of a word or phrase, line or paragraph, from within a quoted text. Four dots are used at the end of a quote to indicate that the original quote continued.

In fiction, an ellipsis is the *dot-space-dot-space-dot-space* you often see in dialogue or narrative. Three dots—no period—are used at the end of a sentence in dialogue when a character is trailing off in thought. Note the space between the last letter and the first dot on the ellipses.

"Seems like only yesterday I was sixteen and dreaming of my first ball gown . . ."

Three dots within a passage of dialogue can be used to indicate a pause in the character's words. This is useful if you want to slow the pace and add a dreamy quality to the character's speech:

"Seems like only yesterday I was dreaming of my first ball gown . . . of course that was before my daddy decided no daughter of his would ever take up dancin'."

Using **Names in Dialogue**

Last year my husband and I watched all the Jesse Stone movies. We loved them, but after a while we noticed something that became downright comical. I'm not sure it was *meant* to be funny, but for the sake of the writers, I hope it was.

In each movie, whenever anyone met the lead character, Jesse Stone, they always said his full name. And in the course of conversation with him, they *continued* to use his name.

Something like this:

"Nice to meet you, Jesse Stone."

"Nice to meet you, Helen."

"Jesse Stone, where was the missing girl last seen?"

"Over at the marina, near the bar."

"Jesse, who saw her there?"

"One of the customers."

"Well, Jesse, was this a reliable witness?"

In real life, how often do you actually say the name of the person you're talking to? Not often, I'd bet. If you're dropping your character's name into dialogue more than once or twice, go back and delete all but the first reference in a scene. The only time you might want to mention a character's name in dialogue is if that character has been missing for several chapters. If so, a casual name drop will remind the reader of who this character is.

Occasionally you might have two or three people involved in a conversation, so you may need to use a character's name if there is no other good way to indicate who is meant. For instance:

> Linda smiled at Joyce and Julie, her best friends. "Imagine seeing you two here," she said, shifting her packages to her other arm. "Julie, did you get a haircut? I love that style on you!"

SPECIAL SITUATIONS

What if you want to write dialogue between a person and a non-human character—an animal, an alien, or something else?

In my book *Unspoken*, my protagonist taught a gorilla to speak sign language. Once I established that Sema, the gorilla, was using her hands to speak, I wrote all her (admittedly brief) dialogue in italics without quotation marks. Once I had established that the italicized lines were Sema's, I didn't have to describe the movements of her hands or even the fact that she was signing. The reader understood.

If you are featuring non-human characters, or humans who don't speak in the conventional way, establish their means of communication and use it consistently throughout the book. You don't want to slow a good passage of dialogue with lots of description of what the reader has already grasped.

The Art of the Zinger

I freely admit that I'm not a natural wit. I can't come up with a verbal zinger in the blink of an eye. But my protagonist can, because as a novelist, I have time to think about what I'd like them to say. The perfect zinger or witticism may not be on the tip of my tongue as I write, but it may come to me later . . . just as in real life, I usually think of the right thing to say a couple of hours after I need the perfect remark.

So if you want your protagonist to snap back with a perfectly timed riposte, if it doesn't come to you in the first draft or even the second, give yourself time to percolate. Chances are you'll find the perfect response, and everyone will marvel at your protagonist's clever wit.

In Conclusion . . .

In summary, *dialogue is what brings a story out of a character's head and sets it in the real world.* Your protagonist, even if he lives alone on Mars or in a bunker underground, will try to communicate with something or someone, and in doing so he will reveal himself. This is what readers hunger for—they read novels to see how the world works and how beings interact with each other. It is through this interaction that we learn and grow.

So make sure your dialogue is appropriate, realistic, and as real as your characters can be—even if they are lying to themselves and others.

Dialogue is the music of a novel. Make sure it sings.

NOTES

CHAPTER 2

1. Ernest Hemingway, "Hills Like White Elephants," https://faculty.weber.edu/jyoung/English%202500/Readings%20for%20English%202500/Hills%20Like%20White%20Elephants.pdf, accessed January 24, 2024.
2. Nathaniel Tower, "How and When to Use Profanity in Your Writing," https://nathanieltower.com/how-and-when-to-use-profanity-in-your-writing/, accessed 10/31/2023.
3. Athol Dickson, personal correspondence.

www.ingramcontent.com/pod-product-compliance
Lightning Source LLC
LaVergne TN
LVHW050029080526
838202LV00070B/6982